Race HORSES

by Michael Sandler

Consultant: Allan Carter, Historian
National Museum of Racing and Hall of Fame
Saratoga Springs, New York

New York, New York

Credits

Cover and Title Page, © Steve Boyle/NewSport/Corbis; 4-5, © AP Images/Amy Sancetta; 6, © Popperphoto/Alamy; 7, © Painting by William Wilson - Maryland Racing Art; 8, © The Hambletonian Society, Inc.; 9, © Paul A. Souders/Corbis; 10, © Jim McCue, Maryland Jockey Club; 11, © Focus on Sport/Getty Images; 12, © AP Images/Kathy Willens; 13, © The Art Archive/Eileen Tweedy; 14, © Karen Givens/Shutterstock; 15, © Dr. William J. Solomon, Pin Oak Lane Farm, New Freedom, PA; 16, © Matthew Stockman/Getty Images/NewsCom.com; 17, © Hoofprints, Inc.; 18, © Tony Triolo/Sports Illustrated; 19, © Bettmann/Corbis; 20, © NYRA/Adam Coglianese; 21, © Ken Regan/Camera 5/Time Inc./Time Life Pictures/Getty Images; 22, © Bettmann/Corbis; 23, © Bettmann/Corbis; 24, © Stan Honda/AFP/Getty Images/NewsCom.com; 25, © AP Images/Al Behrman; 26, © Sabrina Louise Pierce/epa/Corbis; 27, © Dr. William J. Solomon, Pin Oak Lane Farm, New Freedom, PA; 29TL, © Animals Animals/Leonard Rue Enterprises; 29TR, © Bob Langrish; 29BL, © Bob Langrish; 29BR, © Bob Langrish.

Publisher: Kenn Goin
Project Editor: Lisa Wiseman
Creative Director: Spencer Brinker
Photo Researcher: Jennifer Bright
Design: Stacey May

Library of Congress Cataloging-in-Publication Data

Sandler, Michael.
Racehorses / by Michael Sandler.
p. cm. — (Horse power)
Includes bibliographical references and index.
ISBN-13: 978-1-59716-398-9 (library binding)
ISBN-10: 1-59716-398-8 (library binding)
1. Horse racing—Juvenile literature. 2. Race horses—Juvenile literature. I. Title. II. Title: Race horses. III. Series: Horse power (Series)

SF335.6.S26 2007
798.4—dc22

2006029432

For more information, write to Bearport Publishing Company, Inc., 101 Fifth Avenue, Suite 6R, New York, New York 10003. Printed in the United States of America.

10 9 8 7 6 5 4 3 2 1

Contents

All Eyes on Barbaro

The air felt electric. The eager crowd, jammed into the stands, couldn't wait for the 2006 Preakness to begin.

Fans focused their binoculars on one horse—Barbaro. The big chestnut-colored **colt** had **galloped** to a win in each of his first six races.

In horse racing, winning is measured in lengths. Each length is about eight feet (2.4 m)—the distance between a horse's nose and its tail.

Weeks before, Barbaro had shown his talents at the world's most famous horse race, the Kentucky Derby. He ran strong out of the starting gate. He moved steadily through the pack of 20 horses. Then, he rocketed in front to victory.

The Preakness was almost as big a race as the Derby. Would Barbaro be able to do it again?

Barbaro finished the Kentucky Derby in Louisville, Kentucky, with a lead of 6 ½ lengths. It was the biggest victory in 60 years!

A History of Horse Racing

Horse racing is a contest between two or more horses to see which one is fastest. Racing horses isn't new. In fact, it's one of the world's oldest sports.

In about 1500 B.C., people in Asia and North Africa raced horses. Hundreds of years later, **spectators** packed the **Circus Maximus** in ancient Rome. There, they watched horse-drawn **chariots** roar around the **track**.

A Roman chariot race

By the early 1600s, England's first public track opened in London. The sport became so popular that English settlers brought horses and racing to America. At first, wealthy farmers would challenge neighbors to **competitions** between their fastest animals. Soon, regular Saturday races became popular events.

Before there were tracks, early American races could take place just about anywhere.

The first track in America was built on Long Island, New York, in 1665. It was called Newmarket.

Types of Horse Racing

Today, there are many different kinds of horse races. In the United States, the most popular form of the sport is Thoroughbred racing. In these races, **jockeys** sit on top of the horses. They guide the animals around an oval track of dirt or grass.

Harness racing is also very popular. This kind of race also takes place on a track. However, the jockey sits in a sulky. This light two-wheeled cart is attached to the horse with a harness.

The Hambletonian is harness racing's biggest event.

Not all races take place on flat tracks. In steeplechase racing, horses and their riders **navigate** obstacle-filled courses. They jump over stone walls, wooden rails, fences, and ponds.

Each kind of race is a different distance. For example, steeplechases are the longest. They are two miles (3.2 km) or more.

A jockey guides his horse over a fence during the Gold Cup steeplechase in Virginia.

Teamwork

During a race, the horse and his jockey are a team. The horse provides the speed while the jockey guides the animal as they rocket around the track.

Affirmed (right) and Alydar (left) neck and neck at the 1978 Preakness

A jockey's split-second decision can win or lose a race. During the 1978 Preakness, jockey Steve Cauthen was in the lead with his horse, Affirmed. He slowed down the animal, which set the **pace** for the others. This decision also allowed Affirmed to save his energy. Then when jockey Jorge Velasquez tried to push his horse, Alydar, into first place, Affirmed was ready. Well rested, Affirmed was able to flash across the finish line and win the race.

Affirmed won the race by just four inches (10 cm)!

Cauthen and Affirmed celebrating in the winner's circle

Born to Run

Horses, such as those that race in the Kentucky Derby, are all the same **breed**—Thoroughbred. What sets these champions apart from an everyday horse? The answer is good **breeding**. Thoroughbreds are born with special **traits**, such as speed and **stamina**. These animals come from families where their mothers and fathers were probably racehorses themselves.

A Thoroughbred and his jockey

All Thoroughbreds also share a history. They are related to one of three Arabian horses brought to England in the 1700s. Arabians are perfect for racing because they can run long distances. They are also brave and smart.

Byerley Turk was one of the three Arabian horses brought to England in the 1700s.

Other types of races use different breeds. Standardbreds do well in harness racing. Quarter Horses are bred for shorter races, such as the quarter mile (.4 km).

A Young Racehorse

A racehorse begins life like any other horse. On a farm, a young **foal** drinks his mother's milk for four to eight months. He grows taller and stronger. He also plays with the other horses. Before his first birthday, the foal practices getting used to a **bridle**, a saddle, and a rider.

An Arabian mother and her foal

Foals can walk within an hour after they are born.

The most promising **yearlings** are given a trainer who acts as the young horses' teacher. The animals learn to run on an oval track and to **break** from a starting gate. Exercise riders work with the horses to get them into good shape. Like human runners, the horses' strength grows with every workout.

A yearling being saddled for the first time

Race Day

It may take months or even a year before a young horse is ready to race. At the age of two, Barbaro's trainer, Michael Matz, felt the horse was ready for his first competition. Barbaro had been the biggest, fastest yearling on the farm.

Barbaro (left), ridden by an exercise rider, is led by trainer Michael Matz (right) during a morning workout in 2006.

On a crisp afternoon at a track in Delaware, Barbaro and the other horses were led to the **post**. Each horse walked into a stall behind the starting gate. They waited, fidgeting, eager to break free and run.

Then the starter pressed a button. The gate lifted and the horses broke from their stalls. The race was on! Within minutes, Barbaro was the winner.

Barbaro winning his first race in 2005

Like Barbaro, most horses begin racing at age two. Unlike Barbaro, few win their first race!

Triple Crown

Guiding a horse to a Triple Crown victory is the dream of trainers and jockeys. To take the Triple Crown, a horse must win three races—the Kentucky Derby, the Preakness, and the Belmont Stakes. The contests, held over five weeks each spring, are for horses that are three years old.

Seattle Slew won the Triple Crown in 1977. Here he is in action (far right, front) during the Belmont Stakes.

Each of the races varies in length. The Belmont is a long race at 1.5 miles (2.4 km), while the Preakness is shorter at 1 3/16 miles (1.91 km). The Kentucky Derby is somewhere in the middle at 1.25 miles (2.01 km). Only a skilled horse can handle the different tracks and distances equally well. Winning all three races is not an easy job.

Triple Crown winner Citation is considered one of the greatest racehorses ever.

Only 11 horses have ever won the Triple Crown. The most recent winner was Affirmed in 1978.

Super Horse

From 1949 to 1972, no horse was able to win the Triple Crown. Then Secretariat came along in 1973. The chestnut-colored colt with the big white star on his face seemed too pretty. Nobody thought he could end the winless streak. Yet the beautiful horse was frightfully fast. He took the Derby and the Preakness. Only the Belmont remained.

Secretariat streaking to victory in the 1973 Belmont Stakes

At first, the race at Belmont was close. Then Secretariat seemed to shift gears. His legs pumped harder and harder. Soon he was flying, not running. As he pulled 15, 20, then 30 lengths ahead, the other horses became specks in the distance. Secretariat was the new Triple Crown winner.

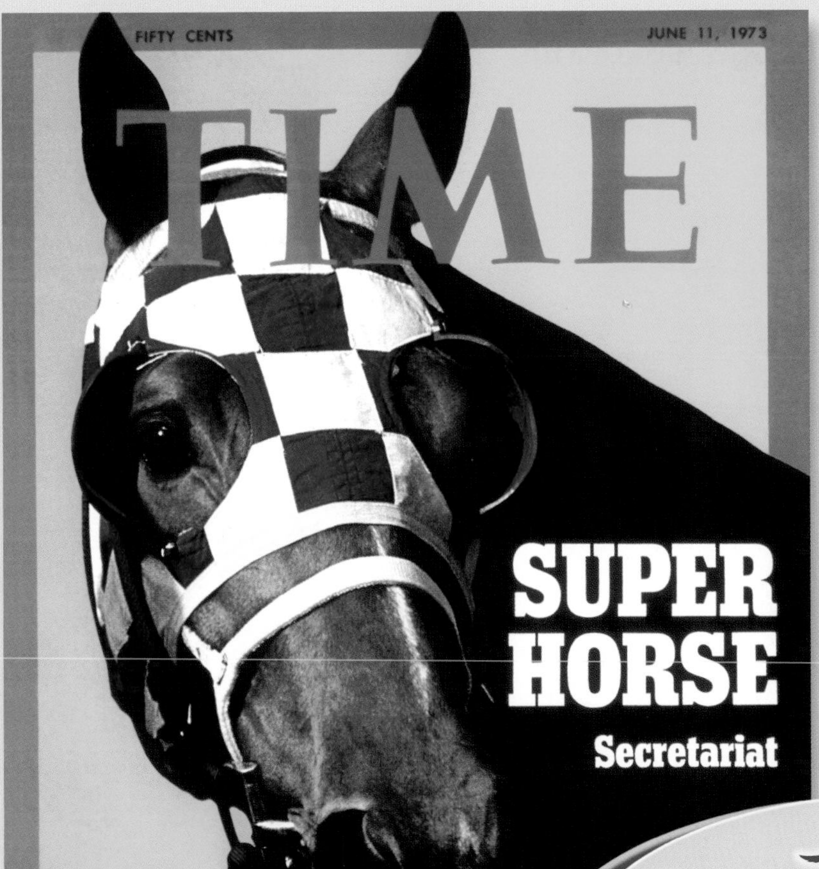
FIFTY CENTS

JUNE 11, 1973

TIME

SUPER HORSE

Secretariat

Secretariat's history-making victory was the sports news story of the year.

Secretariat set a speed record in his Belmont victory. He completed the race in 2:24 minutes. His amazing record remains unbroken today.

Hard Work and Heavy Loads

Racehorses love to run. The sport, however, is extremely demanding. Most horses take part in 10 to 15 races each year.

In some races, the fastest horses must work harder than the others. They carry extra weight, which is called a **handicap**. This weight slows them down and gives the other horses a fairer chance to win.

Man O' War won one race by 100 lengths!

One horse that carried a lot of weight was Man O' War. This mighty champion of the 1920s won 20 out of 21 races. With each victory, his handicap grew bigger. His owner decided to retire him early. He didn't want his horse to carry such heavy loads.

Man O' War with his owner, Samuel Riddle

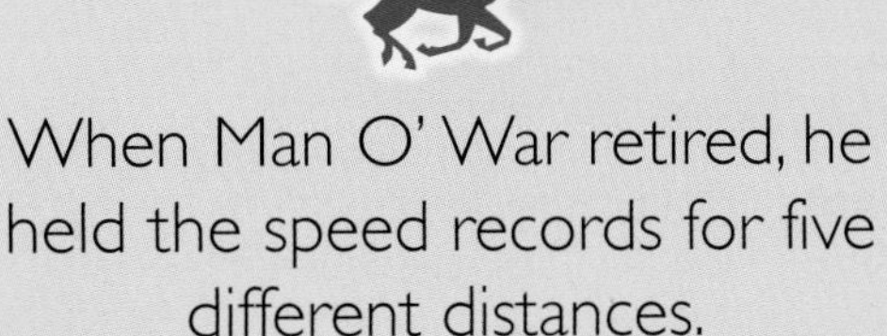

When Man O' War retired, he held the speed records for five different distances.

Tragedy at the Track

Super horses like Secretariat are extremely rare. Barbaro's Kentucky Derby win, however, stirred people's memories. Barbaro reminded people of Secretariat—the way he moved his **forelegs**, the way he took command of a race.

Was Barbaro a super horse, too? He would try to prove it in the 2006 Preakness.

Horses leaving the starting gate at the 2006 Preakness

When the Preakness began, Barbaro thundered from the gate. Yet within seconds, his bid for glory was over. Barbaro and another horse drifted together. Barbaro stepped badly. He reared up in pain. His jockey, Edgar Prado, gently pulled him to a stop. Barbaro's right **hind** leg had shattered in three places. The race for glory was over.

Barbaro after injuring his leg

Barbaro was rushed to an animal hospital. In a five-hour operation, his leg was pieced together with a metal plate and over 20 screws.

The Future

Though racing can be dangerous, few careers end as badly as Barbaro's. Racehorses usually retire healthy after two or three years of competition. Then, they go to a farm to live a more peaceful life.

On the farms, champion horses are visited by fans who have followed them for years. They are also highly sought after for breeding. Breeders hope to pass these Thoroughbreds' skills on to future generations of racehorses.

Jockey Edgar Prado spends time with Barbaro at an animal hospital.

As old favorites retire, new horses emerge to draw the attention of fans. Once in a while, a special young horse arises. People begin to dream: Is this the next Secretariat or Affirmed?

Today, horse racing draws more spectators than any other sport except baseball.

Young fans visit retired racehorses at Pin Oak Lane Farm in Pennsylvania.

Just the Facts

- Who was the greatest champion ever? In 1999, a panel of experts chose Man O' War. They selected him for his incredible speed and nearly perfect record. Secretariat was the runner-up.

- After his death, **veterinarians** examined Secretariat and made a surprising discovery. The great horse's heart was almost three times as large as that of a normal racehorse!

- Many people consider Seabiscuit to be the best racehorse of all time. A **descendant** of Man O' War, Seabiscuit wasn't always a winner. He lost his first 17 races.

- Most champion racehorses are male. However, there have been some very successful female horses. In 1915, Regret became the first **filly** to win the Kentucky Derby. Sixty-five years later, Genuine Risk repeated the feat. The third female horse to win the Derby was Winning Colors in 1988.

- A jockey has to be tough. A fall from a speeding 1,200-pound (544-kg) horse can cause serious injury. Jockey Laffit Pincay, Jr., has the most victories in the history of horse racing. In his career, Pincay has suffered 2 spinal fractures, 11 broken collarbones, 10 broken ribs, and 2 broken thumbs.

Racehorses

Quarter Horse

Thoroughbred

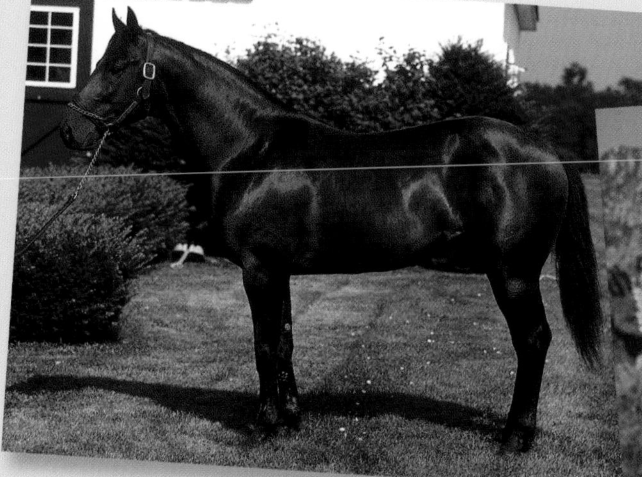

Standardbred

Arabian

Glossary

break (BRAYK) to run as soon as the gate is lifted

breed (BREED) a type of a certain animal

breeding (BREED-ing) the process of keeping animals with special characteristics so that they can mate and produce offspring with those same characteristics

bridle (BRYE-duhl) leather straps fitted to a horse's head and mouth that are used to control and guide the horse

chariots (CHA-ree-uhts) two-wheeled horse-drawn carts

Circus Maximus (SUR-kuhss MAKS-i-muhs) a stadium in ancient Rome built around 600 B.C.

colt (KOHLT) a young male horse that is two years old or younger

competitions (*kom*-puh-TISH-uhnz) contests between people or animals

descendant (di-SEND-uhnt) the child or grandchild of a person or animal

filly (FIL-ee) a young female horse that is two years old or younger

foal (FOHL) a baby horse under age one

forelegs (FOR-legz) a horse's two front legs

galloped (GAL-uhpd) ran at the fastest pace

handicap (HAN-dee-*kap*) weight that horses must carry to give them and other horses a fair chance in a race; the handicap is a combination of the jockey's weight and lead bars carried in the saddle

hind (HINDE) at the back

jockeys (JOK-eez) people who ride horses in a race

navigate (NAV-uh-gayt) to find a way through

pace (PAYSS) a rate of speed

post (POHST) starting point for a horse race

spectators (SPEK-tay-turz) people watching a sporting event

stamina (STAM-uh-nuh) the strength to do something for a long time without getting tired

track (TRAK) a path or course for animals or runners

traits (TRATES) qualities or characteristics of a person or an animal

veterinarians (*vet*-ur-uh-NER-ee-uhnz) doctors who takes care of animals

yearlings (YEER-lingz) racehorses that are one year old

Bibliography

Eisenberg, John. "Off to the Races." *Smithsonian*. 35, no.5 (August 2004).

Handleman, Bill. "From Jersey to Derby." *Asbury Park Press*. May 10, 2006.

Phillips, B. J. "Cauthen: A Born Winner." *Time*. May 29, 1978.

Read More

Baker, Kent. *Thoroughbred Racing*. Philadelphia: Chelsea House (2001).

Budd, Jackie. *The World of Horses*. Boston: Kingfisher (2004).

Libby, Barbara M. *I Rode the Red Horse: Secretariat's Belmont Race*. Lexington, KY: Eclipse Press (2003).

Learn More Online

To learn more about racehorses, visit:
www.bearportpublishing.com/HorsePower

Index

About the Author

Michael Sandler has written numerous books on sports for kids and young adults. He lives in Brooklyn, New York, with fellow writer Sunita Apte and their two children Laszlo and Asha.